Contents

Words in **bold** are in the glossary on page 29.

Seaside walk

Iris, Tanya and Ajwad are planning a walk near their school. They live in Brighton, a city on the south **coast** of England. Their school is called Carlton Hill Primary, and it is to the south of the city, not far from the sea.

The children use different kinds of map to plan the **route** of their walk. They find a **large scale map** of Brighton on the Internet, which shows lots of detail.

The children also look at a tourist map of the seaside city. This map shows them the local **landmarks**.

Iris, Tanya and Ajwad want to find out more about the place where they live. They make a list of questions that they want to answer as they go on their walk.

Focus on History
Brighton has been popular with holiday-makers for over 250 years. It still has a big **tourist industry**.

1. Is there much traffic?

2. What do tourists come to see?

3. What kind of shops are there?

4. What sorts of homes do people have?

5. Are there any parks nearby?

Brighton looks out over the English Channel.

Busy city

Iris, Tanya and Ajwad get ready for their walk. They pack a local map to help them find the way and a **compass** to check the directions they take. They also need a camera and a **pedometer**, to measure how far they walk.

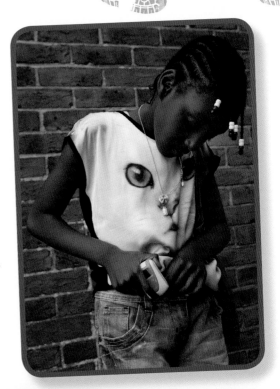

The group leave through the school gates and turn right into Carlton Hill. Soon they turn left, walking south down a road called John Street.

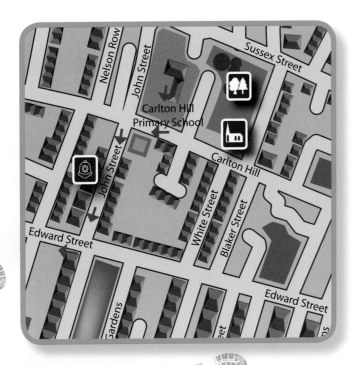

Welcome to
Carlton Hill Primary School
Main entrance
All visitors please report to the office

They go past a big modern office block. This building is only a few years old.

The children come to a **dual carriageway**, which has two lanes going in each direction. This busy road is called Edward Street. The group cross this road at some traffic lights, and pass some shops and offices.

Q: Is there much traffic?

A: Some roads in Brighton have lots of traffic, but there are also some quieter streets in the city.

? Are the roads busy near your school?

EDWARD STREET

Tourist trail

Iris, Tanya and Ajwad stop at a **road junction**, where Edward Street meets the A23, another major road. This section of the A23 is called Pavilion Parade.

Brighton's Royal Pavilion is visited by many thousands of tourists every year.

The children can see the Royal Pavilion on the other side of the road. They cross the road to get a closer look at this unusual palace. It is over 200 years old.

The group looks at a map of Brighton. They can see a picture of the Royal Pavilion on the map. It is one of Brighton's most famous buildings.

Q: What do tourists come to see?

A: Many tourists come to visit the Royal Pavilion.

The group walk down Pavilion Parade into a road called Old Steine. They stop to look at the Brighton War Memorial.

The memorial is for soldiers from Brighton who died during the two World Wars, and in more recent conflicts.

 Is there a **war memorial** near where you live?

On the seafront

Iris, Tanya and Ajwad walk down the road to the sea. They are facing south, and heading towards Brighton Pier. This is another popular **tourist attraction**.

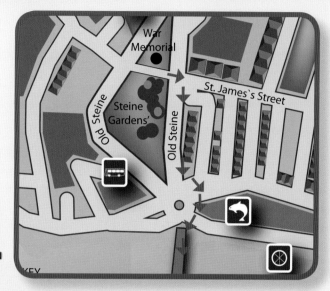

BRIGHTON PIER

*The main road goes all the way down to the **seafront**.*

When the children reach the **pier**, they find it crowded with holiday makers. Food stalls are selling ice creams, candy floss and popcorn, and also fish and chips. There are **amusement arcades** with games and slot machines.

The children walk out along the pier, then stop to look back at their seaside city.

Focus on History

Many people visit Brighton for the day. The train line from London to Brighton was first opened in 1841. **Steam trains** brought **day-trippers** to Brighton and the city soon became known as 'London by the sea'.

They can see a big wheel on the beach. On the other side of the pier, they spot some old buildings on the seafront. These are old tourist hotels. Many of them were built about 150 years ago, during **Victorian** times.

There is a big wheel on the beach, which gives people great views of the coast.

 ? Are there any tourist attractions close to where you live? What are they?

Beach walk

Iris, Tanya and Ajwad go down some steps to get near to the sea. They start looking for shells and pretty stones to take back to school. Iris finds a **cuttlefish** and shows it to her friends.

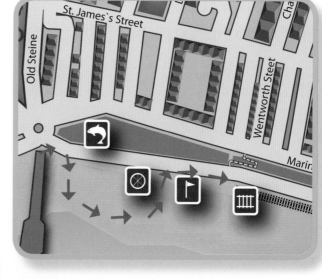

There are lots of things for holiday-makers to do on Brighton Beach. Some people are paddling and swimming in the sea. Others are sunbathing or relaxing in deckchairs. Families and children are playing ball games together.

? How far is it to your nearest beach?
Do you go there often?

There is a big wheel and a crazy golf course on the seafront in Brighton. Tourists can also take rides along the beach on a Victorian electric railway.

VOLKS ELECTRIC RAILWAY
THE OLDEST ELECTRIC RAILWAY IN THE WORLD STILL OPERATING
FREQUENT TRAINS TO AND FROM THE MARINA STATION

Last Train Tonight 5pm

You are about to ride on the world's Oldest Electrical Railway Opened in 1883 Operated by Brighton Council from 1940. (Now Brighton and Hove City Council)

Focus on History
Volk's Electric Railway first opened in 1883. It is the world's oldest working electric railway. It may have to close down because it doesn't make enough money to stay in business.

Holiday shops

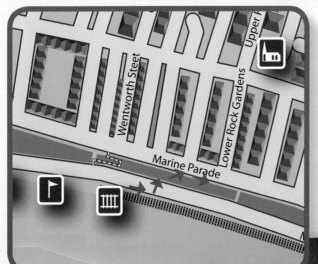

The children leave the beach and go to look at some shops on the seafront. These shops are selling **souvenirs** of Brighton and things to play with at the seaside, such as windmills and beach balls.

Q: What kind of shops are there?

A: The shops near the beach are for tourists.

Iris, Tanya and Ajwad reckon that most of the people they can see on the seafront are tourists. The children do a quick **survey**, asking some passers-by if they live nearby. They all reply they are on holiday, or just visiting Brighton for the day.

The shops on the seafront are for tourists, not local people.

The group climbs some steps towards a road called Marine Parade. This road is **parallel** to the one below. The children walk along, stopping now and then to look down over the beach. They can hear the sound of seagulls above their heads.

The steps near the seafront are very steep.

FOCUS ON SCIENCE
Many **species** of bird live by the sea. The seagull is one of the easiest to spot. Gulls eat fish and other small sea creatures, but they also like to snatch the scraps that people drop.

A common seagull.

City church

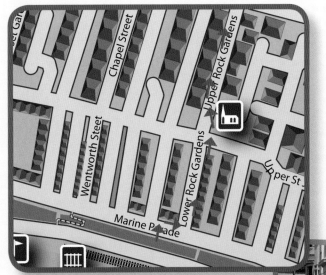

Marine Parade is a busy road with lots of cars and buses driving along it. The children cross over at a **pedestrian crossing**, then turn into a quieter street called Lower Rock Gardens. This road is on a long and steep hill.

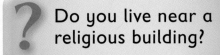

LOWER ROCK GARDENS

Iris, Tanya and Ajwad come to a crossroads. They cross over, passing a church on their right called St Mary's.

*St Mary's Church is a **place of worship** for Christians, but Brighton also has religious buildings for people from other faiths.*

? Do you live near a religious building?

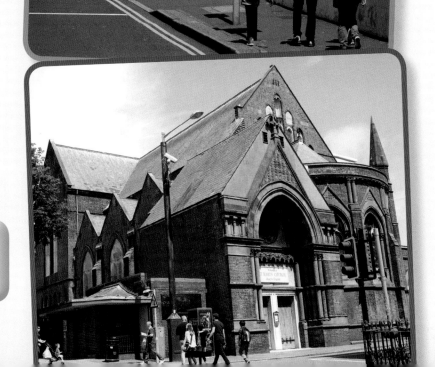

UPPER ROCK GARDENS

The children carry on walking north up the hill, along a road called Upper Rock Gardens.

They walk past some big old houses; some of them are bed and breakfast hotels and holiday homes. Iris, Tanya and Ajwad feel tired as they walk up the hill.

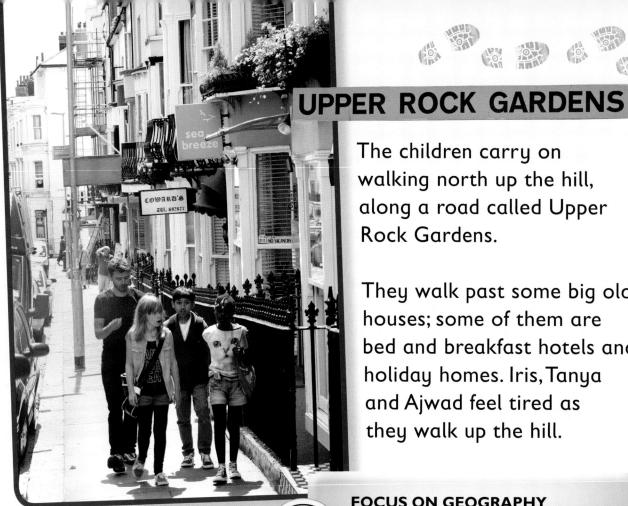

The green hills in the distance are part of the South Downs.

FOCUS ON GEOGRAPHY

The South Downs are chalky hills near the south coast of England. Brighton was built on the South Downs, so this is why the city is so hilly.

Different homes

At the top of Upper Rock Gardens, Iris, Tanya and Ajwad reach a road junction. They turn right into Edward Street, which is the dual carriageway they walked along at the start of their route. Now they are going east, in the opposite direction to before.

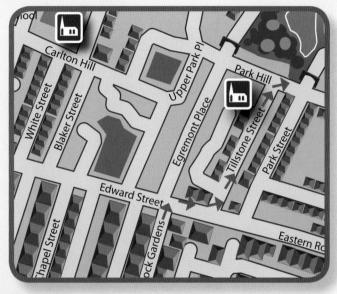

The children walk towards some tall blocks of flats. Tanya says that her nan lives at the top of one of them.

Lots of people live in this part of Brighton.

What sorts of homes do people have?

A: People live in houses and flats. Some homes are big and some are small.

20

TILLSTONE STREET

Brighton & Hove

? Are there many different kinds of homes where you live?

Before the children reach the flats, they turn left into a narrow road called Tillstone Street. They walk past a row of old **terraced houses**, heading north towards a park. This park is called Queen's Park and it is an important green space in the city.

The needle of a compass always points north.

This park dates back to the time of Queen Victoria.

QUEENS PARK

21

In the park

At the top of Tillstone Street, the children turn right and walk towards a tall stone arch. This is Queen's Park Arch, an old entrance to the park. Iris, Tanya and Ajwad go under the arch and through some gates to get into the park.

There is a big pond close to the entrance to the park. The group walks around the pond and spots some ducks, geese and seagulls on the water.

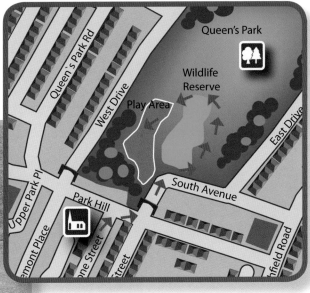

FOCUS ON SCIENCE
The pond in Queen's Park is a small **wildlife reserve**. It is the perfect **habitat** for many different species of insects and birds, such as dragonflies and geese.

Ajwad takes some photos to show to his friends back at school.

Q: Are there any parks nearby?

A: There is a big park with a pond and a children's playground.

There is a playground on the other side of the pond. The children play for a while on the climbing frames, then stop for a drink and a snack. After a quick rest, it is time for them to return to school.

Back to school

Iris, Tanya and Ajwad leave the park and come to another old stone arch. Their teacher gets out his smartphone to see where they are now, using a **GPS** app. The children also look at the tourist map to check their position.

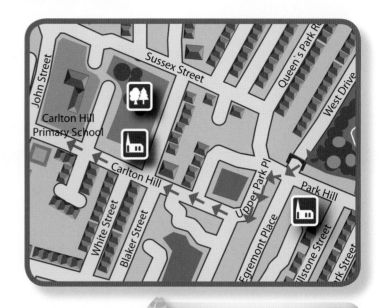

Focus on History

There are two stone arches near Queen's Park. They were built in about 1830, just before Queen Victoria came to the throne.

As the children walk downhill, they look towards the sea. They see some houses and flats, and the Brighton Wheel in the distance. This reminds them that Brighton is not just their home town, but also a fun place to visit.

Soon Iris, Tanya and Ajwad are back at school and their walk is over. Tanya checks her pedometer and discovers they have walked 4.5km that day.

 Do you live in a big town or city?

Working together

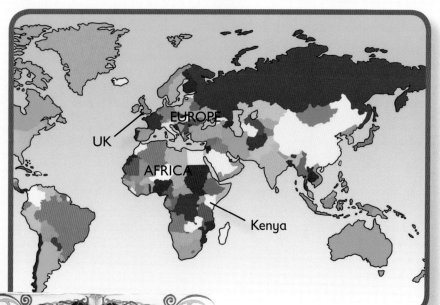

The children at Carlton Hill Primary like to find out about life in other countries. Their school is twinned with a school in Kenya called St Phillip's School. Kenya is a country in Africa.

The children enjoy looking at pictures of their twin school in Kenya.

? Is your school twinned with a school in another country?

A couple of years ago, Iris and her family travelled to Kenya to visit St Phillip's School. They took some presents from Carlton Hill Primary to give to the children and teachers there. Iris made lots of new friends on her trip.

THIS MONTH ON THE FARM
* Plants in greenhouse ✓
* Finish clay oven
* Put up Seedy the Scarecrow ✓
* Make elderflower cordial ✓
* Plant more strawberries ✓
* Weeding

The children at Carlton Hill Primary and St Phillip's School write letters to each other to keep in touch. They also work on exciting projects together. The children at each school are growing local vegetables, so they can swap photos and recipes for cooking them.

FOCUS ON SCIENCE
Kenya has a hotter **climate** than the UK. Farmers in Kenya grow **tropical fruits**, such as bananas and pineapples. In the UK, apples and pears are common fruit crops.

Find the route

Can you follow the whole route on the map?

Find the places shown in photos on the map.

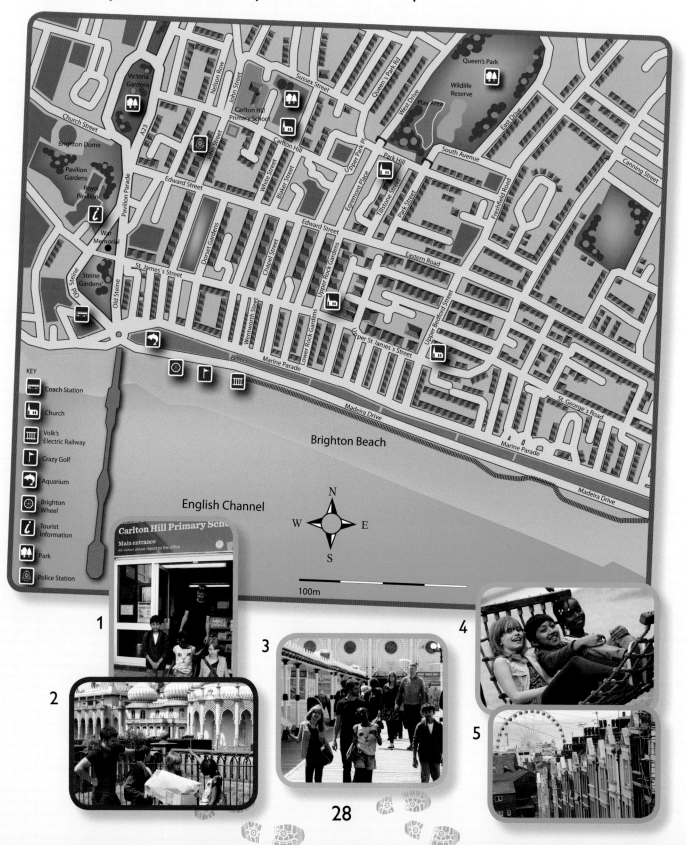

KEY

- Coach Station
- Church
- Volk's Electric Railway
- Crazy Golf
- Aquarium
- Brighton Wheel
- Tourist Information
- Park
- Police Station

English Channel

Brighton Beach

1

2

3

4

5

Glossary

amusement arcade place where you can play on slot machines and video games

climate pattern of weather over a period of time

coast the seashore, and the land close to it

compass instrument that shows you where north is

cuttlefish sea creature in the same family as the squid and octopus

day-tripper person who visits a holiday place for the day

dual carriageway highway with two lanes of traffic on both sides of the road

GPS network of satellites that tells you where you are on Earth

habitat a natural environment or home of a variety of plants and animals

landmark natural or man-made feature that helps you find where you are

large scale map map which shows a lot of detail

parallel going in the same direction

pedestrian crossing place where people can walk across a road safely

pedometer instrument that measures how far you walk or run

pier walkway that stretches out from the shore, over some water

place of worship place where you go to pray and meet people of the same religion

road junction point where two or more roads meet

route way you go to get to a place

seafront part of a seaside town that is next to the beach

souvenir something that reminds you of a place

species a kind of animal or other living thing

steam train train that burns coal to drive a steam engine

survey way of collecting information by asking people a set of questions

terraced houses row of houses that are joined together

tourist attraction place tourists like to visit

tourist industry business to do with holidays

tropical fruit fruit that is grown in countries with a hot climate

Victorian dating back to when Victoria was Queen (1837-1901)

war memorial monument that honours people who were killed in a war

wildlife reserve protected area for animals, birds, insects and plants

Index